CCSS **Genre** Fantasy

☑ W9-AZU-019

Essential Question
What can stories teach you?

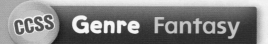

Berries, Berries, Berries

by May Kennedy
illustrated by Sandra Cammell

Chapter 1

Baking Pies

Bear lived in the wild woods.

He was busy baking pies in his den.
Bear had made strawberry pies,
blackberry pies, and cranberry pies.

He was getting ready for the long,
cold winter.

Bear would sleep all winter. When he woke up in spring, he would need lots of food.

Now he wanted to make some blueberry pies.

"Oh no!" cried Bear. "I've run out of berries. I must pick some more."

Bear went to find more berries.
He walked until his feet ached.

But Bear made a terrible discovery.
There were no berries near his den.

Bear sat down under a tree to
concentrate. He had to think of
a plan, and he had to think fast!
There were winter snow clouds in
the sky already.

Bear thought he would go deeper into the woods to look for berries. As he walked along, his stomach began growling and grumbling. He had been so busy cooking that he had eaten nothing all day. He was very hungry.

STOP AND CHECK

What is Bear's problem?

Chapter 2

Friends to the Rescue

As he walked, Bear met his friend Raccoon.

"Good morning, Bear," said Raccoon. "Are you ready for the big sleep?"

"No, I am not!" growled Bear. "I have run out of berries to make my spring pies."

Raccoon was very kind. He wanted to help Bear.

"Pick some apples from the tree near my home," he said.

"Those apples are too sour," said Bear. "Bears like sweet pies."

"Oh," said Raccoon. "Well, good luck with your berry hunting."

Soon Bear met his friend Squirrel.

"Good morning," said Squirrel. "Why is your basket empty?"

"I can't find any berries," said Bear. "Do you have any berries for me?"

"No," said Squirrel. "But I have some walnuts. You can have some."

"Thank you," said Bear. "But I do not want nuts in my pies. They would make the pie crunchy. I will keep searching for sweet berries."

Squirrel and Bear said good-bye to each other. Then they went on their way.

After a lot of effort, Bear realized that there were no berries left.

Suddenly, snow began to fall. Winter was on its way. Bear raced home to his den and put his pies in the cupboard. Then he jumped into bed.

But Bear could not sleep. He was so very hungry.

"Oh dear," said Bear. "I will have to eat my pies. I will have nothing for spring."

But Bear was too hungry to worry about it. He ate up all the pies until at last he felt satisfied. Soon he was fast asleep.

STOP AND CHECK

How did Bear's friends try to help him?

Chapter 3

Spring Supper

Bear slept for many months. The winter snow came and went. Then the first flowers bloomed. Bear woke and let out a big GRRROWL. The growl came from his stomach. He was very, very hungry.

Bear ran into the woods to search for berries. There were berries everywhere, but they were not ripe.

Just then, Raccoon and Squirrel came along. They were going to Skunk's spring party. They were each holding a pie.

"Those pies smell delicious," said Bear.

"Oh, I don't think you would like my sour apple pie," said Raccoon.

"And I am sure you wouldn't like my pie," said Squirrel. "It is made with crunchy walnuts."

When Bear opened his mouth to speak, Raccoon put some apple pie in Bear's mouth.

"Yum, this is good!" cried Bear.

Squirrel waited a moment. Then he gave Bear a piece of walnut pie.

"Wow, walnut pie is great, too," said Bear.

"Aren't you glad we educated you about pies?" said Squirrel.

"I am," Bear said. "My next pies will have new, improved fillings."

Soon the friends arrived at Skunk's party. "Welcome!" said Skunk. "Try a piece of my pie."

"Well, thank you," said Bear. Now that he knew how good his friends' pies tasted, he was inspired to try another new filling.

"What's in this pie?" said Bear as he took a big bite.

"That's my special beetle pie," said Skunk. "Do you like it?"

STOP AND CHECK

Why did Bear change his mind about eating his friends' pies?

Respond to Reading

Summarize

Use details from
Berries, Berries, Berries
to tell what stories
can teach us.

Character	
Wants or Needs	Feelings
Actions	Traits

Text Evidence

1. How do we know that this story is not true? Genre

2. What do we learn about Bear on pages 6 and 7? Character

3. What words help you figure out the meaning of *grumbling* on page 5? Synonyms

4. Write about how Bear changed during the story. Write About Reading

Compare Texts
Read a fable that tells us a story and teaches us a lesson.

The Heron and the Fish

Once there was a heron who lived by a big river.

He spent all day standing still and silent at the edge of the river. He would wait to catch a fish with his long, pointed bill.

One morning, Heron was looking for breakfast.

Small fish swam all around Heron. They thought that he was asleep, but he was only pretending.

"These fish are too small," thought Heron. "I'm going to wait for a big fish to swim by."

He waited and waited... and waited!

Suddenly, all the little fish swam away. Heron couldn't follow them because the water was too deep.

"Gosh," said Heron. "I'm hungry. I should have eaten those small fish."

Poor Heron. The only thing he could find to eat was a tiny snail.

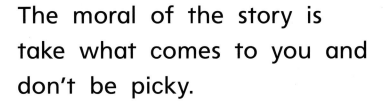

The moral of the story is take what comes to you and don't be picky.

Make Connections

How can stories help us learn from the mistakes of others? **Essential Question**

Compare the ways that the animals learn lessons in these stories.

Text to Text

Focus on Genre

Fables Fables are written to teach an important idea. The talking animals in a fable teach a human or another animal something important.

Read and Find In *The Heron and the Fish* the Heron learns a lesson. What lesson does the Heron learn?

Your Turn

Plan a fable that uses a talking animal to teach a lesson. Choose one part of the story and write it in detail. Remember to use dialogue between the characters to show what is happening.